Neil
ARMSTRONG

Damian Harvey

Illustrated by Mike Phillips

W
FRANKLIN WATTS
LONDON•SYDNEY

Contents

CHAPTER 1
Mad about Planes

Neil Armstrong was born in Wapakoneta, Ohio, USA in 1930. Not many people could afford to fly in aeroplanes...

...so who could have dreamed that one day, Neil would fly all the way to the Moon?

When he was very young,
Neil's father took him to see the
National Air Races in Cleveland.

Neil loved aeroplanes
and he dreamt about
flying in one.

Then, when he was only six years old, Neil's dream came true.

His father took him for an aeroplane ride. The aircraft they flew in was made of metal.

Everyone called it the Tin Goose.

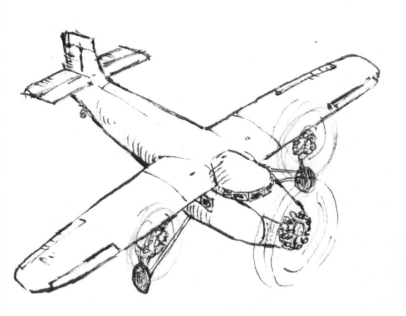

Sitting next to his father, Neil
listened to the roar of the engines
and gazed through the window
at the streets and houses far below.

From that moment on, Neil
wanted to be a pilot.

Neil was shy and wasn't very good at sport, but he loved music and reading.

He also loved building model aeroplanes. He got a job cutting grass so he could buy more models to build.

At night, Neil gazed at the stars and the Moon though their neighbour's telescope.

CHAPTER 2
Up, Up and Away

When he was thirteen, Neil started to have flying lessons. But they were very expensive!

Neil had to get a job baking...

...and work in a shop.

It was boring work but Neil kept on dreaming of flying high above the clouds.

On his sixteenth birthday, Neil got the best present ever – his pilot's licence.

He had learnt to fly even before he could drive a car.

Neil wanted to go to college to
learn about aircraft engineering but
this was also very expensive.

The Navy said they would pay for
him to go if he joined the Navy for
a few years afterwards.

There were lots of pilots in
the Navy so Neil agreed.

Neil worked hard at college but, in 1949, he had to leave half-way through his second year.

The United States of America were preparing for war with Korea and they needed good pilots.

Neil learnt to fly jet fighters that could land and take off from huge aircraft carriers.

During the Korean War, Neil flew into combat 78 times.

After the war, Neil went back to college to finish his studies, but he couldn't wait to get back in the air.

Neil was a brave pilot and was awarded three medals. On one dangerous mission his plane was damaged and he had to eject.

CHAPTER 3
The Race to Space

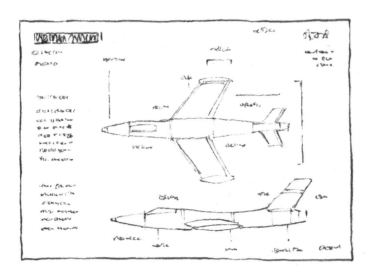

The US government were busy building new kinds of aeroplanes that could fly faster and higher than ever before. The Air Force needed brave pilots to test them. Neil was happy to be one of them.

The most exciting aircraft that Neil flew was the X-15 rocket plane. It could travel at speeds of over four thousand miles an hour. It could even fly up to the edge of space.

From that high the Earth looked like a huge ball...but Neil wanted to fly even higher.

If only they could build an aircraft that could fly up into space!

The Soviet Union and the Americans were racing to send a human into outer space. Then, in 1961, the Soviet Union did it...

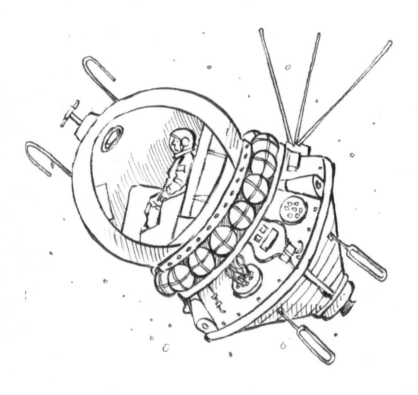

...Yuri Gagarin became the first man in space.

President John F. Kennedy promised that America would beat them by sending a man to the Moon.

John Glenn was the first American in space and Neil was determined to fly there too. But he wasn't the only one.

Hundreds of pilots applied to join NASA (the National Aeronautics and Space Administration) so they could learn to be astronauts. But only nine of them were chosen…

...Neil Armstrong was one of them.

Training to be an astronaut was hard. He learnt how it would feel to be in outer space where there is no gravity.

Neil used a simulator to practise
flying a space capsule.

He even had to learn
how to walk in
a space suit.

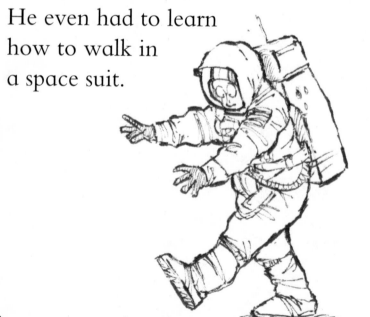

After years of training, Neil was finally ready to go into space.

NASA named him as commander of the Gemini 8 Space Mission. Their mission was to dock with another spacecraft in space.

This was very important if they ever hoped to fly to the Moon.

CHAPTER 4
Docking in Space

On 16th March 1966 an unmanned spacecraft was launched into space.

Later on, Neil Armstrong and his co-pilot, David Scott flew in the *Gemini 8*, launched by the *Titan II* rocket.

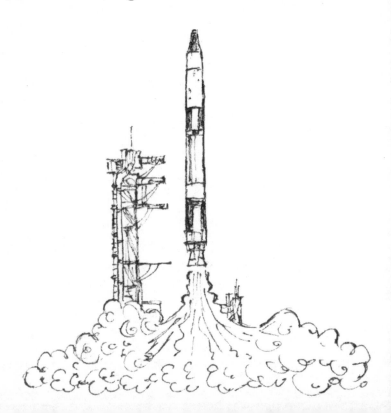

After orbiting the Earth for six and a half hours, Neil and his co-pilot successfully docked *Gemini 8* with the unmanned spacecraft.

Then things started to go wrong...

The spacecraft started spinning out of control.

They knew if they couldn't stop the spacecraft from spinning they would both be killed.

Using all his skill as a pilot, Neil fired the thrusters and slowly the spinning came to a stop.

The two pilots guided the *Gemini 8* spacecraft back towards Earth and made an emergency landing in the Pacific Ocean.

"SPLASH DOWN!"

Then they had to wait to be rescued.

Even though their mission had almost ended in disaster, Neil and David had proved they could dock a spacecraft in space.

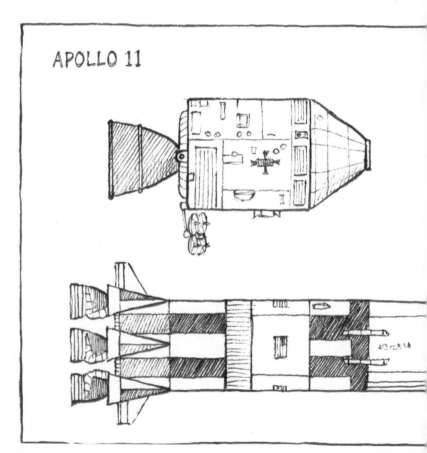

APOLLO 11

NASA were very pleased and they announced that Neil would be captain of the *Apollo 11* mission.

Neil Armstrong was going to the Moon.

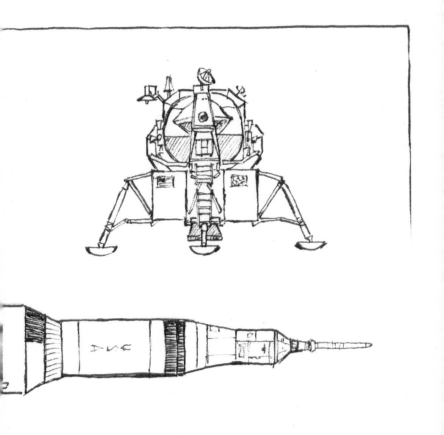

CHAPTER 5
"One Giant Step..."

For the next few months, Neil trained harder than ever before.

He practised flying a lunar module.

He fastened weights to his body and practised walking in water.

Then, on 16th July 1969, Neil Armstrong and his fellow astronauts, Buzz Aldrin and Michael Collins, climbed into their space capsule.

"3...2...1...Zero – We have lift off!"

Millions of people from all over the world watched as the huge rocket roared off into the sky.

In space, the astronauts floated in their spacecraft.

They ate food out of bags and tubes.

They peered at the Earth and
the stars.

They even thought they spotted
a U.F.O.

Then, after flying for three days, the astronauts finally saw the Moon through the windows.

The next day, *Apollo 11* split into two mini spacecraft. Michael Collins stayed behind in the *Columbia* and Neil and Buzz headed for the Moon in the *Eagle*.

Neil saw that the *Eagle* was heading for a bumpy landing so he took over the controls.

On the 20th July 1969, Neil and Buzz landed on the surface of the Moon. They couldn't wait to step outside.

Neil Armstrong was Captain of the *Apollo 11* mission so he was first down the ladder.

The two astronauts had fun walking on the Moon and taking pictures. They also collected rocks and samples to take home.

After returning to Earth, Neil wanted to go and see his family, but he had to wait.

The astronauts spent two weeks in a sealed room to make sure they hadn't brought any germs back from their journey in space.

Then they had to travel around the world. Everyone wanted to hear about their amazing voyage to the Moon.

Neil Armstrong never voyaged into outer space again. He got a job teaching at a University in Ohio.

He even bought a dairy farm where he milked cows and took care of the Earth.

But he will always be remembered as the first person to set foot on the Moon.

When Neil Armstrong died in 2012 President Obama described him as "...among the greatest of American heroes – not just of his time, but of all time."

Timeline

1930   Neil Armstrong is born in Ohio, USA.

1946   Neil gets his first pilot's licence.

1949   Neil flies Navy jets in the Korean War and completes 78 missions.

1955   Neil becomes a test pilot for new aircraft.

1956   Neil marries Janet Shearon.

1957   Russia launched *Sputnik 1*, the first satellite to orbit the Earth.

1961   Russian Yuri Gagarin became the first man to orbit the Earth.

1962   Neil joins NASA as an astronaut.

1966   16th March: Neil Armstrong and David Scott join the *Gemini 8* mission and dock in space.

1969   16th July: *Apollo 11* is launched – Neil Armstrong, Buzz Aldrin and Michael Collins fly to the Moon.

20th July: Neil Armstrong is the first man to walk on the Moon.

24th July: *Apollo 11* successfully lands in the Pacific Ocean near Hawaii.

1971   Neil left NASA and began working at the University of Cincinnati, Ohio as a professor of aerospace engineering.

2012   25th August: Neil Armstrong dies aged 82.

First published in 2014 by
Franklin Watts
338 Euston Road
London NW1 3BH

Franklin Watts Australia
Level 17/207 Kent Street
Sydney NSW 2000

HB ISBN 978 1 4451 3297 6
PB ISBN 978 1 4451 3298 3
Library ebook ISBN 978 1 4451 3300 3
ebook ISBN 978 1 4451 3299 0

Dewey Decimal Classification Number: 920

Series editor: Melanie Palmer
Series designer Cathryn Gilbert

Printed in Great Britain

Franklin Watts is a division of Hachette Children's Books,
an Hachette UK company.
www.hachette.co.uk